# QUICKREADS

LEVEL D • BOOK 1

Elfrieda H. Hiebert, Ph.D.

MW01089705

Glenview, Illinois

Boston, Massachusetts

Chandler, Arizona

Upper Saddle River, New Jersey

ALWAYS LEARNING

PEARSON

**Program Reviewers and Consultants**

**Dr. Barbara A. Baird**
Director of Federal Programs/Richardson ISD
Richardson, TX

**Dr. Kate Kinsella**
Dept. of Secondary Education and Step to College Program
San Francisco State University
San Francisco, CA

**Pat Sears**
Early Childhood Coordinator/Virginia Beach Public Schools
Virginia Beach, VA

**Dr. Judith B. Smith**
Supervisor of ESOL and World and Classical Languages/Baltimore City Public Schools
Baltimore, MD

Acknowledgments appear on page 9, which constitutes an extension of this copyright page.

**Copyright © 2012 Pearson Education, Inc., or its affiliates. All Rights Reserved.** Printed in the United States of America. This publication is protected by copyright, and permission should be obtained from the publisher prior to any prohibited reproduction, storage in a retrieval system, or transmission in any form or by any means, electronic, mechanical, photocopying, recording, or likewise. For information regarding permissions, write to Pearson Curriculum Group Rights & Permissions, One Lake Street, Upper Saddle River, New Jersey 07458.

QuickReads® is a registered trademark of Pearson Education, Inc.

ISBN-13: 978-1-4284-3155-3
ISBN-10:    1-4284-3155-1
15   17

# CONTENTS

# CONTENTS

# CONTENTS

SCIENCE **Animal Communities**

SCIENCE # Birds and Their Habitats

# CONTENTS

SCIENCE

## The Human Body

# Acknowledgments

## Photographs

Every effort has been made to secure permission and provide appropriate credit for photographic material. The publisher deeply regrets any omission and pledges to correct errors called to its attention in subsequent editions.

Unless otherwise acknowledged, all photographs are the property of Pearson Education, Inc.

Photo locators denoted as follows: Top (T), Center (C), Bottom (B), Left (L), Right (R), Background (Bkgd)

**Cover:** Thomas Northcut/Thinkstock; **3** Rue des Archives/©The Granger Collection, NY; **4** ©Michael Ventura/Alamy Images; **5** NASA; **6** ©Justine Evans/Alamy Images; **7** ©William Leaman/Alamy Images; **8** ©Michael Newman/PhotoEdit, Inc.; **10** ©Andre Jenny/Alamy Images; **12** ©North Wind/North Wind Picture Archives; **14** Rue des Archives/©The Granger Collection, NY; **16** ©The Granger Collection, NY; **18** ©Roger L. Wollenberg/UPI/NewsCom; **24** ©Michael Ventura/Alamy Images; **26** National Archives; **28** Craig Brewer/Getty Images; **30** ©David Young-Wolff/PhotoEdit, Inc.; **32** Stockbyte/Thinkstock; **38** ©History/Alamy; **40** NASA; **42** ©Associated Press; **44** Bettmann/Corbis; **46** ©Associated Press; **52** ©Gary Bumgarner/Alamy Images; **54** ©Justine Evans/Alamy Images; **56** ©Harry Engels/Photo Researchers, Inc.; **58** Anup Shah/Thinkstock; **60** ©Gregory G. Dimijian/Photo Researchers, Inc.; **66** ©Craig K. Lorenz/Photo Researchers, Inc.; **68** ©Grant Faint/Getty Images; **70** ©William Leaman/Alamy Images; **72** Photos to Go/Photolibrary; **74** ©Frank Paul/Alamy; **80** ©David Young-Wolff/PhotoEdit, Inc.; **82** ©Michael Newman/PhotoEdit, Inc.; **84** Alan Jackson/©DK Images; **86** ©David Young-Wolff/PhotoEdit, Inc.; **88** Bill Bachmann/PhotoEdit.

# Immigration to America

Immigrants come to the United States from all around the world.

# A Land of Immigrants

Immigrants are people who leave their home country to live in a new country. Except for Native Americans, everyone in your[25] classroom had a family member who was once an immigrant to the United States. Children whose families have lived in the United States for hundreds[50] of years may not have heard about their family members who immigrated. Other children may be immigrants themselves, or they may be the children of[75] people who are immigrants.

Over hundreds of years, immigrants have come to the United States from many different countries. These people may be from many[100] different places, but they all hope to start a new life.[111]

# Immigration to America

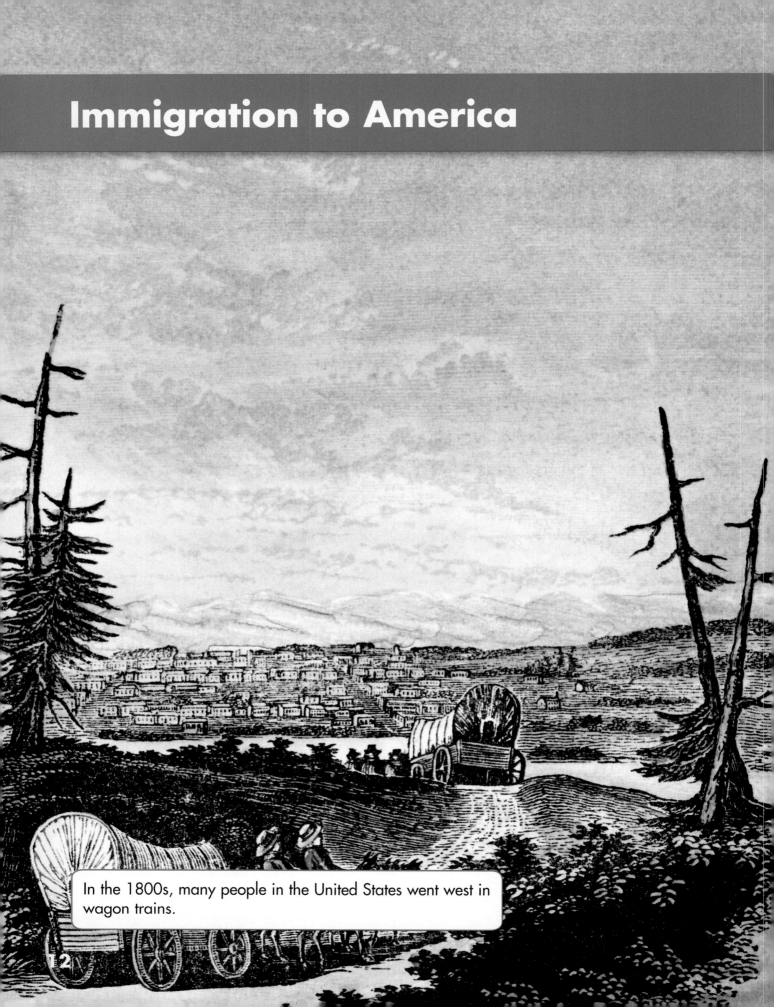

In the 1800s, many people in the United States went west in wagon trains.

# A Land of Opportunity

The United States has often been called the "land of opportunity." Over hundreds of years, people have left their home countries[25] to immigrate to the United States.

Some groups came to America to have the opportunity to practice their beliefs freely. Some came because of the[50] opportunity to have better jobs. Some even came because a few states offered free land to farm.

Some people also were brought to America as[75] slaves. It was many years before the United States offered these people the opportunity to be free.

People still immigrate to the United States. Many[100] people immigrate to have opportunities that they did not have in their home countries.[114]

# Immigration to America

Immigrants on a ship see the Statue of Liberty in New York.

# Getting to America

Until 50 years ago, most immigrants came to the United States in ships. Some ship voyages were difficult, especially for the people[25] who were brought from Africa as slaves.

The voyage could be very hard, even for immigrants who chose to come to the United States. Between[50] 1900 and 1920, 15 million immigrants arrived in ships from Europe. Many of these immigrants were poor. They traveled on the bottom deck of the[75] ship. The bottom deck was often crowded and windowless.

Today, most immigrants to the United States arrive on airplanes. However, immigrants from our North American[100] neighbors, Mexico and Canada, can drive to the United States, or even walk.[113]

# Immigration to America

Many Chinese immigrants first came to Angel Island in California.

# Ellis and Angel Islands

After 1886, the Statue of Liberty greeted ships arriving in New York. Immigrants often cheered when they saw the Statue of[25] Liberty. Many of these immigrants passed through Ellis Island.

First, the immigrants had a health inspection. Some people with serious illnesses were sent back to[50] their home country. People who passed the health inspection were questioned about their background. After this, the immigrants were told if they could stay in[75] the United States.

Inspections of new immigrants who arrived on the West Coast occurred at Angel Island in California. Most of these immigrants were from[100] China. Many Chinese immigrants were kept for a long time at Angel Island.[113]

# Immigration to America

These people are becoming new citizens of the United States.

# Becoming an American Citizen

Most Americans become citizens by being born in the United States. However, every year more than a million immigrants come to[25] the United States. Many immigrants want to become citizens. However, there are certain things people must do to become citizens.

Before 1906, people did not[50] have to know English to become American citizens. Since then, laws have been passed that require everyone who wants to be a citizen to speak,[75] read, and write English. People who want to become citizens must also pass a test about the history and the laws of the United States.[100] Today, only people who know English and pass this test can become American citizens.[114]

Write words that will help you remember what you learned.

## A Land of Immigrants

_____

_____

_____

_____

## A Land of Opportunity

_____

_____

_____

_____

## Getting to America

_____

_____

_____

_____

## Ellis and Angel Islands

_____

_____

_____

_____

## Becoming an American Citizen

_____

_____

_____

_____

# A Land of Immigrants

**1.** The main idea of "A Land of Immigrants" is that _____

    Ⓐ everyone who lives in any country is an immigrant.

    Ⓑ all children in the United States are immigrants.

    Ⓒ people come to the United States to be immigrants.

    Ⓓ someone in most families in the United States was an immigrant.

**2.** What is an immigrant?

_____

_____

_____

# A Land of Opportunity

**1.** Why do some people immigrate to the United States?

    Ⓐ to find out about their past and to have homes

    Ⓑ to find new beliefs and to find their families

    Ⓒ to practice their beliefs and to have better jobs

    Ⓓ to leave the United States and to find their home countries

**2.** Why is the United States often called the "land of opportunity"?

_____

_____

_____

# Review Immigration to America

## Getting to America

**1.** "Getting to America" is MAINLY about _____

    Ⓐ how much immigrants had to pay to get to the United States.

    Ⓑ how difficult it is to get to the United States today.

    Ⓒ how immigrants came to the United States years ago and today.

    Ⓓ the rules for getting to the United States on airplanes.

**2.** Compare how most immigrants came to the United States 50 years ago with how they come today.

_____

_____

_____

## Ellis and Angel Islands

**1.** Another good name for "Ellis and Angel Islands" is _____

    Ⓐ "The Statue of Liberty."

    Ⓑ "Health Inspections in the United States."

    Ⓒ "Living at Ellis Island."

    Ⓓ "Arriving in the United States."

**2.** What happened at Ellis and Angel Islands?

_____

_____

_____

## Becoming an American Citizen

**1.** Many immigrants to the United States want to _____

    Ⓐ become American citizens.

    Ⓑ go to Ellis Island.

    Ⓒ be born in the United States.

    Ⓓ learn about how to be an immigrant.

**2.** What are three things immigrants need to know to become citizens?

_____

_____

_____

## Connect Your Ideas

**1.** What might an immigrant have to do differently in a new country?

_____

_____

_____

**2.** Why do you think immigrants come to the United States today?

_____

_____

_____

# The Constitution of the United States

This family is looking at the United States Constitution.

# What Is the Constitution?

The Constitution is a set of rules for the United States government. One important rule is that the citizens elect the[25] leaders of the government.

The Constitution describes two levels of government, national and state. The national government has certain powers, such as forming an army[50] and navy. The national and state governments share some powers, such as making taxes. The states also have certain powers, such as running the public[75] schools.

The writers of the Constitution knew that the government might need to change as the country changed. These changes are called amendments. The writers[100] gave rules for how amendments to the Constitution could be made.[111]

# The Constitution of the United States

This picture shows the people who signed the United States Constitution.

# We the People

The Constitution starts with the words "We the people." However, when the Constitution was written, more than 200 years ago, these words[25] did not apply to all people. Women did not have all the rights that men had, such as voting in elections. Many African Americans were[50] still slaves. Native Americans were not citizens. Rich people and landowners had more power than poor people.

Over time, four amendments to the Constitution have[75] given the rights guaranteed by the Constitution to all Americans. Today, all people who are citizens can vote in elections. Now the words "We the[100] people" mean that the laws apply to all people equally.[110]

# The Constitution of the United States

The Bill of Rights guarantees that people have certain rights.

# The Bill of Rights

When the Constitution was first put in place, many people believed that the national government might get too strong and force[25] people to do things. These people wanted the Constitution changed to guarantee that people have certain rights.

The first ten amendments were added to the[50] Constitution in 1791. These amendments are called the Bill of Rights because they guarantee that people have certain rights. One right is that Americans are[75] free to practice any religion, or no religion. Americans are also free to speak freely, even if the government does not like what they say.[100] Many countries do not have laws that guarantee people the freedom of religion and speech.[115]

# The Constitution of the United States

This girl is practicing her right to speak freely.

# The First Amendment

People in the United States have rights that are guaranteed by the Bill of Rights. In the Bill of Rights, the First[25] Amendment gives people the right to say and write what they believe. Even when the government does not like a person's opinions, that person may[50] talk and write freely about these opinions.

However, the First Amendment does not mean that people can do anything they want. People cannot break laws[75] and then claim that it is their right to do what they want. Freedom of speech does not mean that one person can tell lies[100] about another person. People may not hurt others, but they can say what they think.[115]

# The Constitution of the United States

Judges make sure that all people are treated fairly.

# The Constitution and the Future

The United States Constitution guarantees certain rights that the government can't take away. The Constitution also was written so that[25] it could be changed as new situations happen in the future.

The Constitution says that when people have different opinions about a situation, they may[50] go to a judge in a court. The judge thinks about the Constitution and sees if other judges have said anything about this situation in[75] the past. Then, the judge decides who is right. If the judge thinks that a law is not fair, the law can be changed. In[100] this way, judges make sure that all people are treated fairly.[111]

Write words that will help you remember what you learned.

### What Is the Constitution?

_____

_____

_____

_____

### We the People

_____

_____

_____

_____

### The Bill of Rights

_____

_____

_____

_____

### The First Amendment

_____

_____

_____

_____

### The Constitution and the Future

_____

_____

_____

_____

## What Is the Constitution?

**1.** Which of these is in the Constitution?

    Ⓐ the school you must go to

    Ⓑ the work your parents must do

    Ⓒ the national government you must vote for

    Ⓓ the powers of national and state government

**2.** What is the Constitution?

_____

_____

_____


## We the People

**1.** "We the People" is MAINLY about how _____

    Ⓐ the meaning of "We the People" has changed.

    Ⓑ immigrants to America became citizens.

    Ⓒ amendments can be made to the Constitution.

    Ⓓ different groups of people came to live in the United States.

**2.** How has the meaning of "We the People" changed since the Constitution was written?

_____

_____

_____

## The Bill of Rights

**1.** Why did people want to have a Bill of Rights?

Ⓐ They wanted to have laws in the United States.

Ⓑ They wanted to be able to vote for their government.

Ⓒ They wanted to guarantee that people have certain rights.

Ⓓ They wanted to make sure that immigrants could become citizens.

**2.** What is the Bill of Rights?

_____

_____

_____

## The First Amendment

**1.** Another good name for "The First Amendment" is _____

Ⓐ "An Important American Right."

Ⓑ "Amendments to the Constitution."

Ⓒ "How People Made Amendments to the Constitution."

Ⓓ "Why People Want to Vote for their Government."

**2.** What right does the First Amendment give to people in the United States?

_____

_____

_____

## The Constitution and the Future

**1.** The main idea of "The Constitution and the Future" is that _____

    Ⓐ laws were written to ask questions about the Bill of Rights.

    Ⓑ the Constitution of the United States can't be changed.

    Ⓒ laws can be changed as new situations happen.

    Ⓓ the Constitution is rewritten every year.

**2.** What happens when people have different opinions about what rights mean?

_____

_____

_____

## Connect Your Ideas

**1.** Why do you think it is important for the United States to have a Constitution?

_____

_____

_____

**2.** Why might it be important to be able to change the laws of a country?

_____

_____

_____

This is a stamp with a picture of Benjamin Banneker.

# Benjamin Banneker

Benjamin Banneker was an African American man who had his own farm when slavery was still allowed in the United States. During the [25] day, Benjamin Banneker was a farmer. At night, he studied science.

Benjamin Banneker was interested in astronomy, the science of stars and planets. He learned [50] so much about astronomy that he wrote an almanac. An almanac is a book that uses astronomy to predict the weather. Farmers used his almanac [75] to decide when to plant crops.

Benjamin Banneker also believed that one person can make a difference in the world. To try to make a [100] difference for others, Benjamin Banneker wrote letters to America's leaders asking that slavery be stopped. [115]

# American Pathfinders

Ellen Ochoa is getting ready to fly on the space shuttle *Discovery*.

# Ellen Ochoa

Ellen Ochoa was an astronaut who flew on the space shuttle *Discovery*. One of her inventions was used on the space shuttle to[25] get better pictures of Earth from space. Ellen Ochoa showed that she has skills beyond those of an astronaut and an inventor. On the space[50] shuttle *Discovery*, she played songs on her flute.

Ellen Ochoa is a Latin American woman who became a scientist, inventor, and astronaut. When she visits[75] children in schools, Ellen Ochoa says that she owes her success to a good education. Ellen Ochoa says, "Education allows you to be outstanding. It's[100] a matter of working hard to get a good education."[110]

Franklin D. Roosevelt often spoke to the American people over the radio.

# Franklin D. Roosevelt

When Franklin D. Roosevelt became president in 1933, times were hard. Many banks had closed. Millions of people had lost their jobs.[25]

President Roosevelt started many programs that helped people get jobs.  Then, World War II began. In 1941, the United States entered the war. President Roosevelt[50] helped lead the countries that were fighting for their freedom. In 1945, the United States and its partners won the war.

President Roosevelt used a[75] wheelchair because his legs had been weakened by an illness he had before he became president. The American people liked that President Roosevelt faced any[100] challenge. He was the only person to win the presidency four times.[112]

Maya Lin is holding a model of her design for the Vietnam Veterans Memorial.

# Maya Lin

Maya Lin was only 21 years old when she won the national contest to design the Vietnam Veterans Memorial in Washington, D.C. Her[25] design for the Vietnam Veterans Memorial is simple. The names of the 58,000 Americans who died in the Vietnam War are written on two long[50] walls of polished black granite.

At first, some people did not like Maya Lin's design. The polished black granite memorial had none of the people[75] or flags that most memorials have. Now, people praise the memorial. As visitors touch the names of those who died, they see their own faces[100] in the polished granite. Visitors remember the memorial that Maya Lin designed.[112]

# American Pathfinders

Rachel Carson's book *Silent Spring* showed that DDT was a danger to many animals and to people.

# Rachel Carson

Not long ago, farmers used a chemical called DDT to kill insects that were hurting their crops. Rachel Carson wrote a book that[25] said that this chemical was killing other animals, not just insects. She said that DDT was a danger to animals and people. She called her[50] book *Silent Spring* because she believed that many animals would die from DDT. Nature would be silent if farmers kept using DDT.

When Rachel Carson[75] wrote *Silent Spring*, she knew that farmers and makers of the chemical DDT would be angry. She didn't know that the president would read her[100] book, but he did. Soon, there were laws to control the use of DDT.[114]

Write words that will help you remember what you learned.

## Benjamin Banneker

_____
_____
_____
_____

## Ellen Ochoa

_____
_____
_____
_____

## Franklin D. Roosevelt

_____
_____
_____
_____

## Maya Lin

_____
_____
_____
_____

## Rachel Carson

_____
_____
_____
_____

## Benjamin Banneker

**1.** Benjamin Banneker believed that _____

    Ⓐ one person can make a difference in the world.

    Ⓑ new kinds of crops can be planted in many places.

    Ⓒ one person can predict how the stars and planets will move.

    Ⓓ almanacs could be used to study science.

**2.** How would you describe Benjamin Banneker?

_____

_____

_____

## Ellen Ochoa

**1.** "Ellen Ochoa" is MAINLY about _____

    Ⓐ how Ellen Ochoa got an education.

    Ⓑ the problems Ellen Ochoa had on the space shuttle.

    Ⓒ how Ellen Ochoa invented the space shuttle.

    Ⓓ the talents and skills of Ellen Ochoa.

**2.** Why does Ellen Ochoa think that she became successful?

_____

_____

_____

# Review American Pathfinders

## Franklin D. Roosevelt

1. Another good name for "Franklin D. Roosevelt" is _____
   Ⓐ "A President Who Got Jobs for People."
   Ⓑ "Winning the War."
   Ⓒ "A President Who Faced Any Challenge."
   Ⓓ "Working from a Wheelchair."

2. Tell about two important things that President Roosevelt did.

   _____

   _____

   _____

## Maya Lin

1. Which of these things did Maya Lin do?
   Ⓐ She designed the Vietnam Veterans Memorial.
   Ⓑ She wrote the Vietnam veterans' names on the memorial.
   Ⓒ She passed the law to get the Vietnam Veterans Memorial built.
   Ⓓ She became a veteran of the Vietnam War.

2. How is Maya Lin's memorial different from other memorials?

   _____

   _____

   _____

## Rachel Carson

**1.** "Rachel Carson" is MAINLY about how Rachel Carson _____

    Ⓐ wrote a letter to the president.

    Ⓑ wrote a book that helped control the use of DDT.

    Ⓒ passed a law against DDT.

    Ⓓ made a chemical that farmers could use on their crops.

**2.** What did Rachel Carson think that DDT did?

_____

_____

_____

## Connect Your Ideas

**1.** What is a pathfinder?

_____

_____

_____

**2.** Tell about someone you know or have read about that you think is a pathfinder.

_____

_____

_____

# Animal Communities

Squirrels live in communities only when they are young.

# Two Kinds of Animal Communities

Many animals, such as squirrels, live near one another. Squirrels mate with one another, then the mother squirrel takes care[25] of her young for the first few months of their lives. After that, squirrels are on their own. Squirrels do not stay together, so their[50] animal communities, or groups, are not permanent.

Other kinds of animals do live in permanent communities. These communities help animals stay safe and find food.[75] The kinds of permanent animal communities vary. Some communities, such as those of ants, may have thousands of members. Other communities, such as those of[100] beavers, may have only the three to five members of one family.[112]

# Animal Communities

This chimpanzee is using a rock as a tool to break a nut.

# Chimpanzee Clans

Chimpanzees belong to groups of 30 to 70 members called clans. Chimpanzees move around the forest in smaller groups that are part of[25] their clan. Each group has one male, two or three females, and their young. These groups teach and protect young chimpanzees.

It takes six years[50] for young chimpanzees to learn all they need to know. Young chimpanzees learn how to use sticks and stones as tools. They learn which fruits[75] and insects to eat. Young chimpanzees learn the sounds that clan members use to give one another information. Because chimpanzees make a new place to[100] sleep every night, knowing how to make a nest quickly is also important.[113]

# Animal Communities

Lodges are safe places for beaver families to live.

# A Beaver Lodge

Most rodents, such as squirrels, live on their own. One exception is the prairie dog. Prairie dogs live in large permanent communities.[25] Another exception is the beaver. Beavers live in small permanent communities. Also unlike other rodents, beavers move slowly on land and quickly in the water.[50]

Beavers need to live near water, but they can't live in it like fish. Beavers solve this problem by building dams across streams. Beavers cut[75] down trees with their teeth and move the branches in their mouths. In the calm pond behind the dam, beavers build homes called lodges. A[100] beaver lodge is the home for one male, one female, and their young.[113]

# Animal Communities

Male lions can guard their pride from other animals.

# A Pride of Lions

Lions are the only big cats that live in large groups. A group, called a pride, has two or three male[25] lions, as many as 15 female lions, called lionesses, and their cubs. As a group, lions can defend their homes and hunt large animals like[50] antelope. Antelope are bigger and faster than lions, but a group of lions can trap an antelope.

Unlike other big cats, male lions, with their[75] huge manes, differ in appearance from lionesses. Because male lions are slower than lionesses, lionesses do most of the hunting for the pride. Male lions[100] use their fierce appearance and loud roar to guard their pride from other animals.[114]

# Animal Communities

These ants are getting food for the other ants in their colony.

# A Colony of Ants

Most types of ants are tiny. However, ants live successfully in almost every place on Earth, except in frozen areas. Ants[25] are successful because they live in highly ordered communities called colonies. Each ant has a particular job in the colony. The queen lays eggs. Once[50] the male ants mate with the queen, their job is done and they die.

Most of the ants in a colony are worker ants that[75] do many jobs. Only female ants are workers. Worker ants build the nest for the colony and care for the young. They find food for[100] the colony. In addition, worker ants defend their colony from attacks by other ant colonies.[115]

# Review Animal Communities

Write words that will help you remember what you learned.

## Two Kinds of Animal Communities

_____

_____

_____

## Chimpanzee Clans

_____

_____

_____

## A Beaver Lodge

_____

_____

_____

## A Pride of Lions

_____

_____

_____

## A Colony of Ants

_____

_____

_____

## Two Kinds of Animal Communities

**1.** The main idea of "Two Kinds of Animal Communities" is that _____

    Ⓐ all animals live in large groups.

    Ⓑ animals live in different kinds of communities.

    Ⓒ scientists study animal communities.

    Ⓓ communities help animals take care of their young.

**2.** How can animal communities be different?

_____

_____

_____

## Chimpanzee Clans

**1.** Why are clans important to chimpanzees?

    Ⓐ Clans help young chimpanzees find their way home.

    Ⓑ Clans have many male and female chimpanzees.

    Ⓒ Clans find the forest where chimpanzees live.

    Ⓓ Clans teach and protect young chimpanzees.

**2.** Name three things young chimpanzees need to know.

_____

_____

_____

# Review Animal Communities

## A Beaver Lodge

1. Another good name for "A Beaver Lodge" is _____
   - Ⓐ "Beavers are Rodents."
   - Ⓑ "Beavers Live on Their Own."
   - Ⓒ "How Beavers Live."
   - Ⓓ "Beaver Dams."

2. Retell what you learned in "A Beaver Lodge."

   _____

   _____

   _____

## A Pride of Lions

1. "A Pride of Lions" is MAINLY about _____
   - Ⓐ how lions guard their pride from other animals.
   - Ⓑ the fierce appearance and loud roar of lions.
   - Ⓒ how lions live.
   - Ⓓ how lionesses trap antelope.

2. How do male and female lions look and act differently?

   _____

   _____

   _____

## A Colony of Ants

**1.** Why can ants live successfully almost anywhere on Earth?

    Ⓐ Ants are very small.

    Ⓑ Ants do not need much food.

    Ⓒ Ants can do many jobs in their colony.

    Ⓓ Ants live in ordered communities.

**2.** What is an ant colony?

_____

_____

_____

## Connect Your Ideas

**1.** How does living in a community help an animal?

_____

_____

_____

**2.** Name three ways animal communities are different from one another.

_____

_____

_____

# Birds and Their Habitats

Burrowing owls make their homes in holes that other animals have dug.

# Habitats of Birds

The 800 kinds of birds in North America have many different habitats. A habitat is the usual area in which a particular[25] kind of plant or animal lives. The habitats of many birds are in wooded areas, but different birds select particular kinds of trees. Nuthatches live[50] in pine trees, while blue jays live in thick bushes.

The habitats of other birds are on or over water. Seabirds, such as terns, come[75] to land only to mate and hatch their young. The habitats of other birds, such as burrowing owls, are in grasslands. Burrowing owls make their[100] homes in burrows or underground holes that small animals have dug and left.[113]

Canada geese fly a long way when they migrate.

# Birds That Migrate

When the days get shorter in the fall, many birds leave their homes in the north to fly south to their winter[25] homes. They spend the winter in places that are warm and where food is easy to find. This travel from one home to another is[50] called migration.

Some birds make long migrations. Canada geese fly almost 2,000 miles. Ruby-throated hummingbirds are only about $3\frac{1}{2}$ inches long. However, these tiny[75] hummingbirds migrate almost as far as the much larger Canada geese. Arctic terns make the longest migration of all. Arctic terns spend their summers close[100] to the North Pole and their winters close to the South Pole.[112]

# Birds and Their Habitats

These birds are keeping warm by trapping air in their feathers and by huddling together.

# Birds in Cold Weather

Some birds do not migrate. Instead, they live all year in places with cold winters. These birds have ways to stay $^{25}$ warm in winter. Birds like gray jays flutter their wings to trap air in their feathers. This air acts as padding that keeps gray jays $^{50}$ warm. Chickadees have soft, fine feathers close to their skin. On the coldest days, chickadees huddle together in tree holes to stay warm.

Other birds $^{75}$ hide food during the summer and fall. In winter, blue jays eat acorns they have hidden. Nuthatches eat the parts of bugs they have put $^{100}$ under tree bark. This hidden food helps birds live during the cold winter. $^{113}$

# Birds and Their Habitats

Some birds care for their young in nests that they make in trees.

# Nests

Birds make nests to protect their eggs until they hatch. Once their eggs hatch, birds use their nests to care for their young. The[25] nests of birds are as different as their habitats.

Birds that live on or near water, such as grebes, build nests on floating plants in[50] ponds and lakes. Flycatchers build nests in tree holes. Barn swallows build mud nests that they stick on high ledges of buildings. The nests of[75] killdeers are hardly nests at all. Killdeers use a hollow in the ground.

Not all birds build nests. Cowbirds lay their eggs in the nests[100] of other birds. Young cowbirds are raised by the birds that built the nest.[114]

# Birds and Their Habitats

Some city birds make their nests on the tops of poles.

# City Homes for Birds

As cities get bigger, the woods disappear that were some birds' habitats. Some of these birds have learned to live in [25] cities. Finches like to live in the poles of traffic lights. The heat of the traffic lights keeps them warm.

Pigeons that once lived on [50] cliffs now make their homes in the rafters of buildings or on statues. At night, barn owls fly around cities. During the day, they rest [75] under highway overpasses.

Snowy owls have chosen strange winter homes. Each fall, they travel from the North Pole to the landing fields of airports in [100] northern cities. The roar of jets does not seem to bother them. [112]

# Review Birds and Their Habitats

Write words that will help you remember what you learned.

## Habitats of Birds

_____

_____

_____

_____

## Birds That Migrate

_____

_____

_____

_____

## Birds in Cold Weather

_____

_____

_____

_____

## Nests

_____

_____

_____

_____

## City Homes for Birds

_____

_____

_____

_____

## Habitats of Birds

**1.** Another good name for "Habitats of Birds" is _____

    Ⓐ "Kinds of Birds."

    Ⓑ "Birds in Trees."

    Ⓒ "Where Birds Live."

    Ⓓ "Grasslands and Trees."

**2.** What is a habitat?

_____

_____

_____

## Birds That Migrate

**1.** When birds migrate, they _____

    Ⓐ travel from one home to another.

    Ⓑ fly to their nests.

    Ⓒ find new places to get food.

    Ⓓ fly to places to have their young.

**2.** What is migration?

_____

_____

_____

# Review Birds and Their Habitats

## Birds in Cold Weather

**1.** "Birds in Cold Weather" is MAINLY about _____

    Ⓐ the many kinds of birds.

    Ⓑ how to stay warm the way birds do.

    Ⓒ what birds eat after they migrate to their new homes.

    Ⓓ how some birds live in places with cold winters.

**2.** How do birds stay warm and find food during cold winters?

_____

_____

_____

## Nests

**1.** The main idea of "Nests" is that _____

    Ⓐ all birds make their nests in trees.

    Ⓑ birds have many different kinds of nests.

    Ⓒ all birds' nests look alike.

    Ⓓ all birds use each other's nests to lay their eggs.

**2.** What are three places that birds build nests?

_____

_____

_____

## City Homes for Birds

**1.** What are some places where city birds live?

    Ⓐ  in traffic lights and on statues

    Ⓑ  under highway overpasses and on cliffs

    Ⓒ  on statues and in barns

    Ⓓ  in woods and on the landing fields of airports

**2.** Why have some birds learned to live in cities?

_____

_____

_____

 **Connect Your Ideas**

**1.** Compare the habitats of two birds in this topic. How are they different?

_____

_____

_____

**2.** Where might you see bird homes in your neighborhood?

_____

_____

_____

# The Human Body

The many systems of this girl's body work together to help her talk and write.

# The Systems of the Human Body

People use some tools and machines, such as pens, that are simple. Other tools, such as cars, are complex.[25] However, no machine is as complex as the human body.

Inside your body are systems that have special jobs. The job of one system is[50] to keep you breathing. Another system moves blood throughout your body. Another system gives your body shape and support so that you can move. Another[75] system processes the food you eat. In all, 10 different systems do the work of your body. All of these systems are hidden but one.[100] This system covers all of the other systems. It is your skin.[112]

Sweating helps people keep their bodies cool.

# The Perfect Container

Human skin is the perfect container for the body's other nine systems. Cardboard and plastic, which are often used for containers, cannot[25] do what human skin does. The six pails of water that a body holds would seep through cardboard or tear through plastic.

Skin stops many[50] germs from getting inside the body. Skin also helps to keep the body's temperature from going up or down too much. If it's hot, people[75] sweat. Sweat draws heat from the body. As the sweat dries, the body cools down. When it's cold, people shiver and get goosebumps. Goosebumps happen[100] when pores in the skin close. The closed pores help keep heat inside the body.[115]

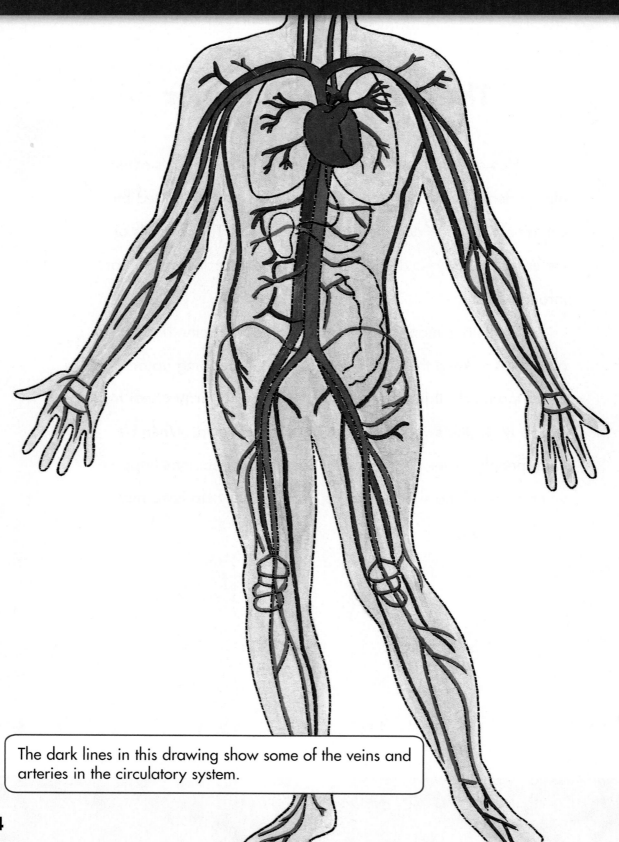

The dark lines in this drawing show some of the veins and arteries in the circulatory system.

# The Circulatory System

The tiny blue lines that you can see through your skin are part of your body's circulatory system. The circulatory system keeps[25] blood flowing throughout your body. The heart is the pump that keeps your blood moving.

Veins and arteries are the tubes that carry the blood.[50] Red blood that is rich in oxygen runs through the arteries to all parts of the body. Veins carry blood back to the heart. The[75] blood in the veins looks blue because some of the oxygen is gone. Once this blood is pumped through the heart and lungs, it is[100] full of oxygen again, and it is ready to circulate through the body.[113]

# The Human Body

This woman's eyelids and lashes help keep her eyes clean.

# The Body's Repair Kit

The human body is designed to keep germs out. Skin forms a protective covering over the systems inside the body. Where [25] there are openings in the skin, the body has ways to protect itself. For example, lids and lashes keep the eye clean. Both hairs in [50] the nose and wax in the ears catch germs.

When germs do get in, the human body uses its own repair kit. White blood cells [75] protect the body from illness by gobbling up harmful germs. The body also repairs cuts. Blood dries up and forms a clot, or scab, over [100] the cut. New skin grows under the hardened scab, repairing the cut. [112]

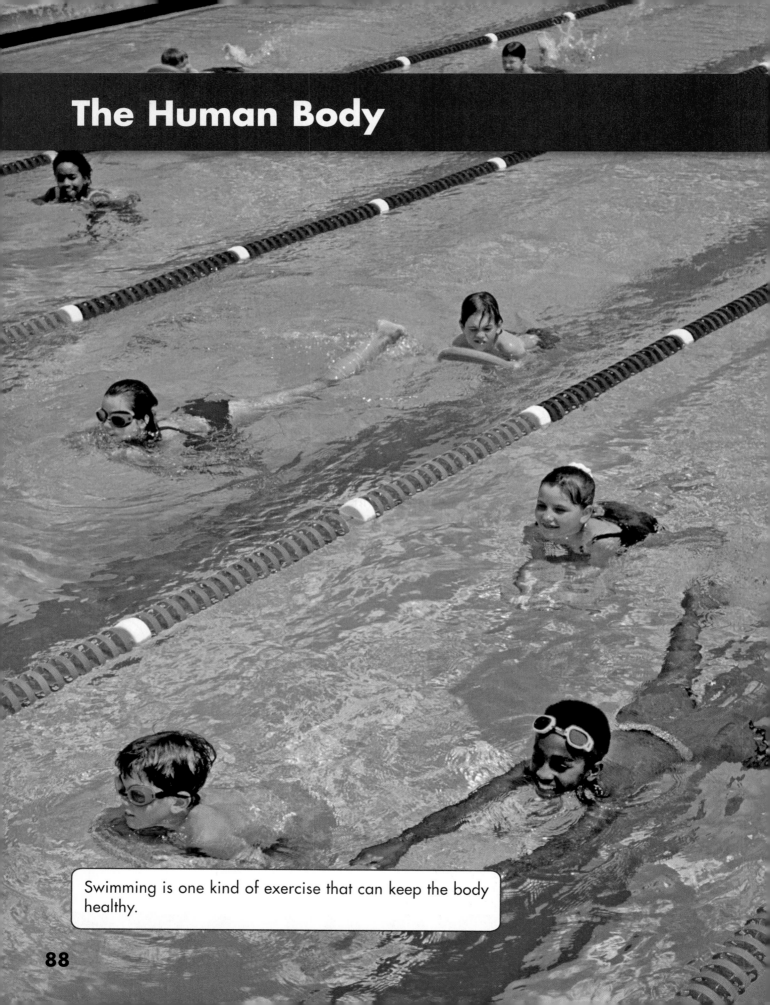

# The Human Body

Swimming is one kind of exercise that can keep the body healthy.

# Keeping the Body Going

The human body can repair itself, but it does need help from its owner. Human bodies need the right food to [25] stay healthy. When people eat the right mixture of foods, they have energy to learn, work, and play. Because more than half of the body [50] is water, people need to drink plenty of water.

The human body also needs sleep and exercise. The body's systems restore their energy during sleep. [75] Exercise makes the heart and lungs strong. Strong hearts and lungs get energy and oxygen to the muscles quickly. Some ways to make your heart [100] and lungs stronger are by riding a bike, dancing, walking, and swimming. [112]

Write words that will help you remember what you learned.

## The Systems of the Human Body

_____

_____

_____

_____

## The Perfect Container

_____

_____

_____

_____

## The Circulatory System

_____

_____

_____

_____

## The Body's Repair Kit

_____

_____

_____

_____

## Keeping the Body Going

_____

_____

_____

_____

## The Systems of the Human Body

**1.**   "The Systems of the Human Body" is MAINLY about _____
   Ⓐ the breathing system in the human body.
   Ⓑ the systems that help the human body work.
   Ⓒ how to use simple and complex tools and machines.
   Ⓓ the systems of all living things.

**2.**   What are four jobs that the human body's systems do?

_____

_____

_____


## The Perfect Container

**1.**   Another good name for "The Perfect Container" is _____
   Ⓐ "Human Skin."
   Ⓑ "Cardboard and Plastic."
   Ⓒ "Keeping the Body Cool."
   Ⓓ "Stopping Germs."

**2.**   Retell what you learned in "The Perfect Container."

_____

_____

_____

## Review The Human Body

### The Circulatory System

**1.** Which are part of the circulatory system?

    Ⓐ the veins and arteries

    Ⓑ the skin and veins

    Ⓒ the oxygen and blood

    Ⓓ the body's tubes and skin

**2.** What does the circulatory system do?

_____

_____

_____

### The Body's Repair Kit

**1.** How does the body protect itself?

    Ⓐ with the veins and arteries of the circulatory system

    Ⓑ by using all of its systems to gobble up harmful germs

    Ⓒ by keeping germs out or repairing itself

    Ⓓ with openings in the skin, eyes, nose, and ears

**2.** How does the body repair itself?

_____

_____

_____

## Keeping the Body Going

1. The main idea of "Keeping the Body Going" is _____
   - (A) how much food people need to eat.
   - (B) how the body repairs itself.
   - (C) how people can make their hearts stronger.
   - (D) how people can keep their bodies healthy.

2. Name three things a person can do to keep the body going.

_____

_____

_____

## Connect Your Ideas

1. How is the human body like a machine?

_____

_____

_____

2. Describe two systems that are working in your body now.

_____

_____

_____

# Reading Log • Level D • Book 1

| | I Read This | New Words I Learned | New Facts I Learned | What Else I Want to Learn About This Subject |
|---|---|---|---|---|
| **Immigration to America** | | | | |
| A Land of Immigrants | | | | |
| A Land of Opportunity | | | | |
| Getting to America | | | | |
| Ellis and Angel Islands | | | | |
| Becoming an American Citizen | | | | |
| **The Constitution of the United States** | | | | |
| What Is the Constitution? | | | | |
| We the People | | | | |
| The Bill of Rights | | | | |
| The First Amendment | | | | |
| The Constitution and the Future | | | | |
| **American Pathfinders** | | | | |
| Benjamin Banneker | | | | |
| Ellen Ochoa | | | | |
| Franklin D. Roosevelt | | | | |
| Maya Lin | | | | |
| Rachel Carson | | | | |

| | I Read This | New Words I Learned | New Facts I Learned | What Else I Want to Learn About This Subject |
|---|---|---|---|---|
| **Animal Communities** | | | | |
| Two Kinds of Animal Communities | | | | |
| Chimpanzee Clans | | | | |
| A Beaver Lodge | | | | |
| A Pride of Lions | | | | |
| A Colony of Ants | | | | |
| **Birds and Their Habitats** | | | | |
| Habitats of Birds | | | | |
| Birds That Migrate | | | | |
| Birds in Cold Weather | | | | |
| Nests | | | | |
| City Homes for Birds | | | | |
| **The Human Body** | | | | |
| The Systems of the Human Body | | | | |
| The Perfect Container | | | | |
| The Circulatory System | | | | |
| The Body's Repair Kit | | | | |
| Keeping the Body Going | | | | |

# Self-Check Graph

Column headers (left to right):
A Land of Immigrants · A Land of Opportunity · Getting to America · Ellis and Angel Islands · Becoming an American Citizen · What Is the Constitution? · We the People · The Bill of Rights · The First Amendment · The Constitution and the Future · Benjamin Banneker · Ellen Ochoa · Franklin D. Roosevelt · Maya Lin · Rachel Carson · Two Kinds of Animal Communities · Chimpanzee Clans · A Beaver Lodge · A Pride of Lions · A Colony of Ants · Habitats of Birds · Birds That Migrate · Birds in Cold Weather · Nests · City Homes for Birds · The Systems of the Human Body · The Perfect Container · The Circulatory System · The Body's Repair Kit · Keeping the Body Going

Row values (y-axis): 150, 148, 146, 144, 142, 140, 138, 136, 134, 132, 130, 128, 126, 124, 122, 120, 118, 116, 114, 112, 110, 108, 106, 104, 102, 100, 98, 96, 94, 92, 90, 88, 86, 84, 82, 80, 78, 76, 74, 72, 70

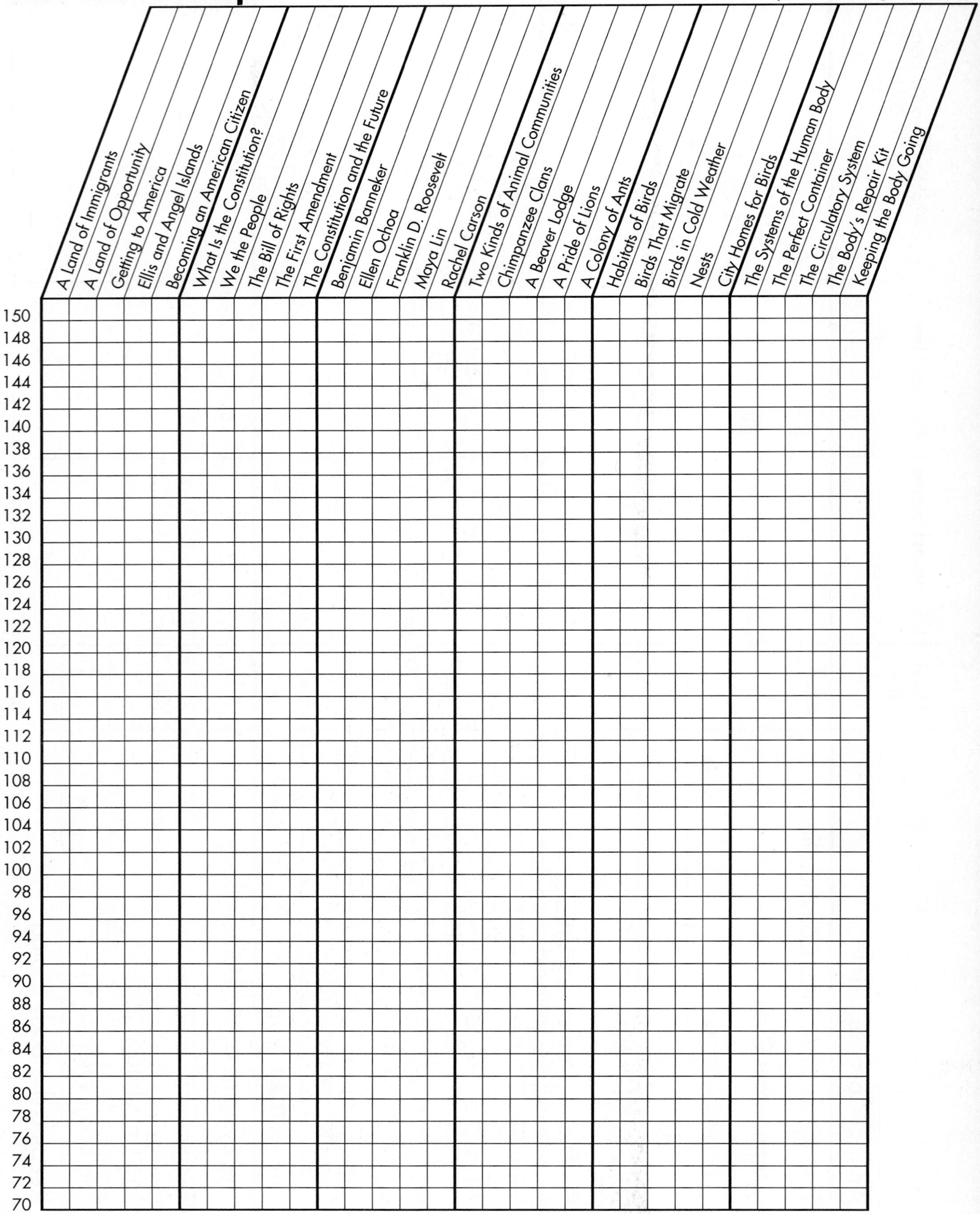

GW00859531

CHRISTMAS 2021

To Rory.
happy Reading
and Learning
about birds
love,
Granny and
Grandad.

# Little Godwit finds his Wings

Emily Lim-Leh

Illustrated by John Lim

**Marshall Cavendish**
Children

In the icy cold Arctic, one last egg sat alone. Unhatched. Left-behind.

Finally, one day...

Little Godwit peered out and saw Owl.
"Have you seen my family?" he asked.

"You're late," Owl said.
"Your family has flown far south by now."

Little Godwit looked up and saw the moon beaming at him. He fluttered his wings to fly.

"Stay!" Owl said. "I'll make you a hunter."

Little Godwit hunted in his thin, feathery coat.
He shivered in the cold wind.

He pounced on his prey.
But he was off-target.

Without a hunter's eye, Little Godwit caught only frostbite.

I'm not made to hunt like Owl, he thought.

Little Godwit wandered away and found a flock of cranes preparing to fly south.

"Can I follow you?" he asked.

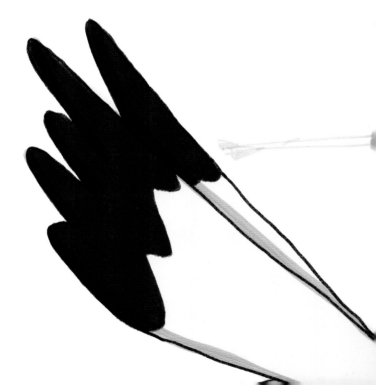

"Sure, if your tiny wings can keep up," the cranes said.

Flip, flap, flutter. Little Godwit flapped hard to follow the cranes.

The cranes tired out from flying and landed next to a gleaming river.

Little Godwit was charged with energy from the flight and wanted to go on.

"Stay!" the cranes said.
"We'll make you a dancer."

Little Godwit tried to spin and shake a leg.
He bumped against a crane to his left and
poked another to his right.

"Follow our footwork!" the cranes trumpeted.

Without an in-born dance rhythm, Little Godwit bobbed out of step.

*I'm not made to dance like the cranes*, he thought. *Am I made to do anything well?*

Little Godwit hobbled straight into kingfishers getting ready to fly further south.

"Can I follow you?" he asked.

"Sure, hover along," the kingfishers said.

Flip, flap, flit. Little Godwit flitted alongside the kingfishers.

As he was about to zoom ahead, the kingfishers landed on a small island.

"Stay!" the kingfishers said.
"We'll make you a diver."

Little Godwit beat his wings hard to stay in position.
He plunged in and crashed into a rock.

"Keep practising!" the kingfishers chorused.

Without a diver's body, Little Godwit flopped on his belly every time.

*I cannot dive like the kingfishers,* he thought.

*What on earth am I made to do?*

Little Godwit looked up and caught the moon beckoning to him. He fluttered his wings and took off.

Flip, flap, zip.

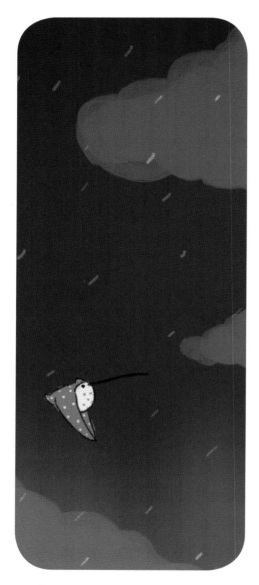

Little Godwit flew south, guided by the stars at night...

...and the sun in the day.

He steered where tailwinds blew him along.

Little Godwit flew
non-stop for days.

He grew lighter
and mounted higher.

*I wonder if I can reach
the moon,* he mused.

After gliding over a long stretch of sea,
Little Godwit searched for a landing spot.
He wheeled around in the air and spied a nearby coast.

He flew nearer and saw that it was dotted with birds.
So, he called out.

The ground stayed silent.

"Should I stay?" Little Godwit wondered aloud

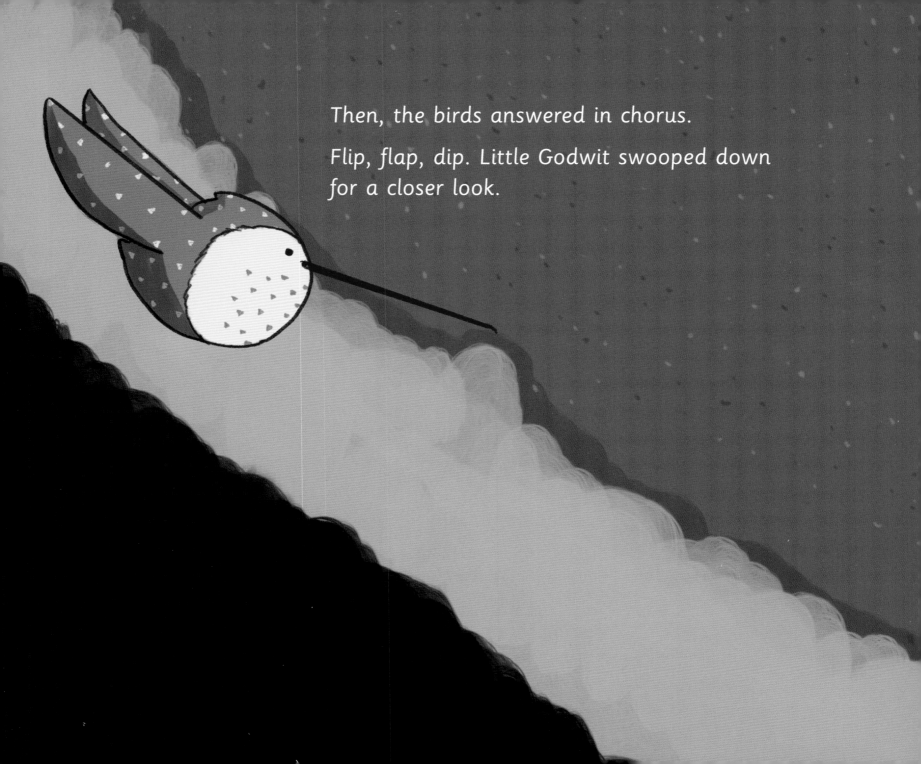

Then, the birds answered in chorus.

Flip, flap, dip. Little Godwit swooped down for a closer look.

Godwits covered the entire coast!

Little Godwit's heart soared as he landed.

"You're late, son!" an old Godwit said.
"I'm glad you found your wings to get here."

"So am I!" Little Godwit said. "Do you always fly here?"

"Yes! I've flown non-stop from the Arctic to this land
of the kiwis every year of my life," the old Godwit replied.
"Do you think all this flying will get me to the moon?"

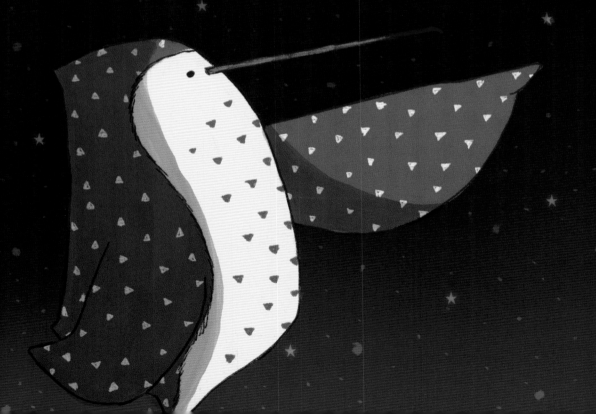

"I believe so," Little Godwit said with wide-eyed wonder.
*We're made to fly as far as the moon.*

## Let's Discuss

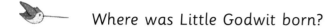 Where was Little Godwit born?

Where was Little Godwit's family?

What did Owl try to teach Little Godwit?
Could Little Godwit be like Owl?

What did the cranes try to teach Little Godwit?
Could Little Godwit keep up with the cranes?

What did the kingfishers try to make Little Godwit do?
Could Little Godwit copy what the kingfishers did?

Where did Little Godwit find his flock?

What did Little Godwit finally discover he was good at?

What amazing thing do godwits do every year?

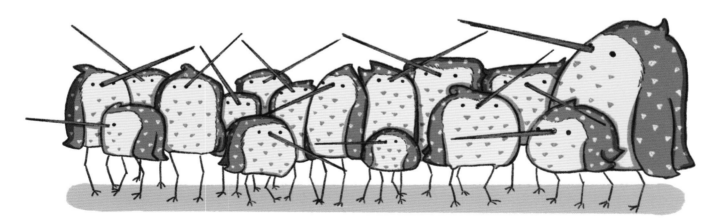

## More About Bar-tailed Godwits

The bar-tailed godwit is a brownish shorebird. It has a long tapering bill and a white tail that is barred with brown bands. Its appearance seems ordinary, but it is an incredibly awesome bird!

### Did You Know?

- Bar-tailed godwits hold the world record for the longest non-stop flight. They can fly for eight to nine days without stopping to eat or drink!

- Bar-tailed godwits fly from the Arctic (where they breed) to Australia and New Zealand (to escape the cold winter). Before they go, they eat enough to build up large stores of fat for energy to fly.

- As the bar-tailed godwit does not eat during the long flight, it doesn't need its digestive organs. These organs shrink, so the bird can fly with less weight.

- An estimated 325,000 bar-tailed godwits make the epic journey across the world from the Arctic to South East Asia, Australia and New Zealand to escape the winter every year.

- With a total round-trip distance of 29,000 km, it is likely that bar-tailed godwits will fly more than 460,000 km during their lifetime. That is more than the distance between the earth and the moon!

Scan these QR codes to find out more about the bar-tailed godwit.

BirdLife Australia

BirdLife International

New Zealand Birds Online

Wildscreen Arkive

## The Bar-tailed Godwit's Flight Details

In the story, Little Godwit detours from the migration route that bar-tailed godwits use to fly from the Arctic to New Zealand. In his journey of self-discovery, Little Godwit follows other flocks and also stops over in two places. These locations are actually along the flight route that bar-tailed godwits take when they fly from New Zealand back to the Arctic. Check out the route that bar-tailed godwits take in their epic migration journey in the map below.

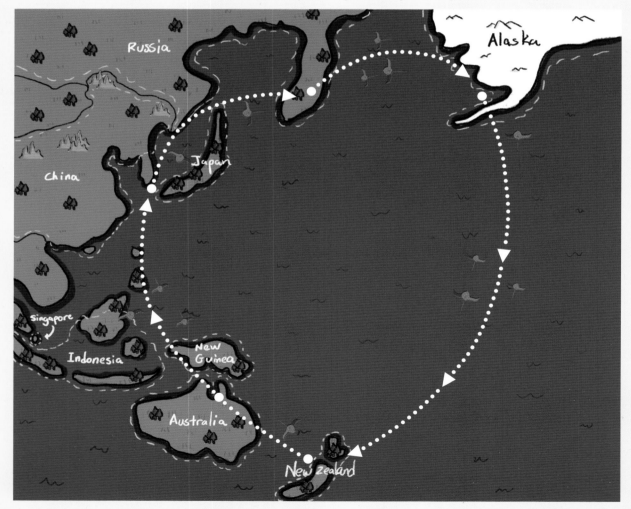

Scan the QR code to read more about the bar-tailed godwit's flight route.
https://teara.govt.nz

## About the Author

Award-winning author Emily Lim-Leh was hatched in Singapore. She is the first outside North America to win three medals for children's books at the IPPY awards (the world's largest book awards) and also the first in South East Asia to win the Moonbeam Children's Book Award. Like Little Godwit, Emily took a somewhat lonesome journey to find her wings as an author. Now, Emily's imagination happily takes flight in search of new tales to write.

Scan the QR code to read more about Emily.
https://mummumstheword.wordpress.com

## About the Illustrator

John Lim was born and bred in Singapore. Also known as SeeSaw, John is a dreamer. He loves to illustrate and doodle as it helps him express his inner thoughts better than words. Like Little Godwit, John is always willing to try new things. He believes that we should not be afraid to be ourselves and express our ideas, and that we should have fun doing it!

Scan these QR codes to find out more about John. http://seesaw.work/ and https://www.instagram.com/see_n_saw/

*For Caleb, Isabelle and Annabel*
*May God grant you the stamina and inner compass*
*of a godwit in your journey of life.*

*~ E.L*

Text © 2019 Emily Lim-Leh
Illustrations © 2019 John Lim

Published by Marshall Cavendish Children
An imprint of Marshall Cavendish International

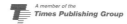

A member of the
**Times Publishing Group**

All rights reserved

No part of this publication may be reproduced, stored in a retrieval system or transmitted,
in any form or by any means, electronic, mechanical, photocopying, recording or otherwise,
without the prior permission of the copyright owner. Requests for permission should be addressed to
the Publisher, Marshall Cavendish International (Asia) Private Limited, 1 New Industrial Road, Singapore 536196.
Tel: (65) 6213 9300 E-mail: genref@sg.marshallcavendish.com Website: www.marshallcavendish.com/genref

The publisher makes no representation or warranties with respect to the contents of this book,
and specifically disclaims any implied warranties or merchantability or fitness for any particular purpose,
and shall in no event be liable for any loss of profit or any other commercial damage,
including but not limited to special, incidental, consequential, or other damages.

Other Marshall Cavendish Offices:
Marshall Cavendish Corporation. 99 white Plains Road, Tarrytown NY 10591-9001,USA •
Marshall Cavendish International (Thailand) Co Ltd. 253 Asoke, 12th Flr, Sukhumvit 21 Road, Klongtoey Nua,
Wattana, Bangkok 10110, Thailand • Marshall Cavendish (Malaysia) Sdn Bhd, Times Subang, Lot 46,
Subang Hi-Tech Industrial Park, Batu Tiga, 40000 Shah Alam, Selangor Darul Ehsan, Malaysia.

Marshall Cavendish is a registered trademark of Times Publishing Limited

**National Library Board, Singapore Cataloguing-in-Publication Data**

Name(s): Lim, Emily, 1971- | Lim, John, illustrator.
Title: Little godwit finds his wings / Emily Lim-Leh; Illustrated by John Lim.
Description: Singapore: Marshall Cavendish Children, 2019.
Identifier(s): OCN 1066062991 | ISBN 978-981-48-4117-7 (hardcover)
Subject(s): LCSH: Godwits--Juvenile fiction. | Birds--Juvenile fiction. | Self-actualization (Psychology)--Juvenile fiction.
Classification: DDC 428.6--dc23

Printed in Malaysia